MIRACLES

Remembering God's Interventions in my Family

Elizabeth Moll Stalcup

Healing Center
INTERNATIONAL

For more information about Healing Center International, please visit our website: www.GodHealsToday.org.

ISBN: 9798650877738

Content

Many of these accounts were written long ago, closer to the time they happened. Then they languished on my computer, until the coronavirus of early 2020 made me realize that I had left them in the shadows for far too long. I sensed God whispering to my heart, *Tell your children. Remind your family, and yourself, of the times I intervened in your common life*. It is easy to lose faith and become discouraged. I pray that these accounts, ones that I know are true because they happened to me and my family, will lift your spirits and help you to trust that God has you. He is with you. He is still a miracle worker.

CHAPTER 1

THE BOOT IN THE ROAD

Winter 1994

There is just one way to bring up a child in the way he should go, and that is to travel that way yourself.

—ABRAHAM LINCOLN

Are not two sparrows sold for a penny? Yet not one of them will fall to the ground apart from the will of your Father. And even the very hairs of your head are all numbered. So don't be afraid; you are worth more than many sparrows.

—MATTHEW 10:29-31

Where was Sarah's other boot?

"Sammy," I yelled downstairs to my eight-year-old son, "go get Sarah's boot for me. It's in the car." We were running late.

A minute later he dashed up the stairs. "Mom, I can't find it."

Oh, bother, I thought, *how come no one else in this family can find anything?* I was positive that boot was in the car. Sarah had been wearing her snow boots when we went out the night before.

I rushed downstairs to the garage and flung open the car door. But the boot wasn't there. *Oh well,* I thought, exasperated. *I'll find it later. We've got to go.*

"Everybody in the car," I ordered. Fortunately, Sarah, age three, was just going along for the ride. I carried her to the car and strapped her in her car seat. Once I got the older kids to school, I would find her missing boot.

But when we got home, I couldn't find it. I searched everywhere. "God," I asked, "please show me where Sarah's boot is." In my mind I saw a picture of a lonely stretch of highway. We had driven on that road last night on our way to a Christmas party.

I shook my head. Sarah's boot on the road? I didn't think so.

I recalled the drive. Sarah had been riding in the front seat next to my husband. I was in the back with our two older kids.

Back in the 1990s it was okay to have your child in a car seat in the front seat. I often let Sarah ride in front because she spent so much time in the car while I drove her older siblings to basketball practice, ice-skating lessons, school, and church activities. Sammy and Mina complained when I moved their little sister's car seat up front, but I felt that letting her sit next to me was a small concession for the hours she spent riding in the car.

That night we had been in a hurry. In the rush, we had left Sarah's car seat up front rather than take time to move it to the back seat.

But that night, Sarah was in no mood for another ride in the car. She started fussing, then kicking and screaming. I tried to restrain her from the back seat, but I couldn't calm her from there. When she landed a hard kick on my husband's elbow, sending our car into the next lane, my husband pulled over onto the side of the road.

Furious, I flung open the door on Sarah's side of the car, unbuckled her car seat and ordered her to climb to the back seat. She obeyed silently, stepping between the front bucket seats to the back. Then I yanked the car seat out of the car and threw it in back, where my older daughter, Mina, strapped it in.

How could her boot have fallen out? I wondered. *It couldn't have,* I reasoned. *She never even got out of the car!*

I prided myself on being a meticulous person. That night I had been standing between the car door and Sarah the entire time it was open. Surely, I would have noticed if her boot had fallen out near my feet.

I waited three days. The weather was cold and rainy. We missed those boots. Even worse, because I had recently lost my job, we didn't have the money to buy new ones.

Every time I prayed and asked God to show me where the boot was, I saw the same stretch of dark highway. I was getting more and more agitated. *Was God speaking to me?* I had to look. Even if the boot wasn't there, at least I'd be able to accept the loss and move on.

I called my husband at work. "I know this sounds crazy, but do you remember where we pulled over on the highway the other night?"

He laughed when I told him my plan. "I'm not sure, but I think it was just south of Braddock Road."

I loaded Sammy, his friend Nick, and Sarah in the car. Twenty minutes later we were on the highway. When I passed the Braddock Road exit, I slowed the car.

"Look carefully," I ordered. "See if you can spot Sarah's purple snow boot."

None of us saw a boot.

Soon Popes Head Road loomed in view.

I exited, made a U-turn, and headed home. *I can't believe I came down here to look,* I thought. *This is absurd!*

Then I remembered. I had told Nick's mother that we were going to look for Sarah's boot because I thought God had told me it was on the highway! *When will I learn to keep my mouth shut?* I wondered. *Now I will have to tell her that I have an overactive imagination!*

As we drove home, I glanced across the highway. Something purple was lying on the other side of the road, four lanes away. *Could it be the boot?*

"I see it, I see it!" shouted Nick from the back seat of the car.

That clinched it. Nick thought he saw it, too!

I turned the car around at the Braddock Road off-ramp and headed south again. "All three of you look carefully," I said. I glanced back. Three small noses were plastered against the window.

Even though it was mid-day and traffic was light, I wasn't comfortable driving slower than 45 mph on the busy highway. We covered the distance in no time. Once again, no boot.

"Okay," I said, "this is getting ridiculous! We're going home. I can't believe I wasted time doing this."

But as I pulled back onto the highway headed home, I was sure I saw the boot across the highway in the distance again.

Oh no, I thought. *I'm going nuts! And driving in circles.*

I had to go back and look one more time.

This time when I got back on the highway, I pulled off the road onto the paved shoulder. I turned on my flashing hazard lights and drove 10 mph.

About a half mile later, Nick suddenly shouted, "There it is!"

I slowed to a stop. Right in front of the car was a purple boot lying on its side with the tan lug sole facing the road.

Nick hopped out of the car and scooped up the boot. He held it high waving it back and forth as he jumped up and down.

When he got back to the car, Sarah hugged the boot to her chest. The kids bounced up and down on the back seat. "We found it, we found it," they chorused.

That summer, Sarah's feet grew too big for the purple boots. We passed them down to a little girl in our church family. When we see them flash by at the end of her sturdy legs, we still laugh. God knew that boot was on the road, and he tried to tell me, too. But it took him a long time to convince me. I had to drive in circles, until I learned to slow down enough to see what God knew was there all along.

*****

What is God trying to show you that you are going to have to slow down to see?

Dear Lord,

I'm rushing from one place to another. Slow me down, Lord. Calm my frantic heart that thinks I have to do it all. Cause me to rest in in the shadow of your wings, to listen to your voice, and to do only what you are calling me to do.

In Jesus' name, Amen.

~ CHAPTER 2 ~

STREP HOUSE

Spring 1997

I consider that our present sufferings are not worth comparing with the glory that will be revealed in us.

—PAUL, ROMANS 8:18 (NIV)

You are quite willing to have a cross, but you want to choose it yourself; you would have it common, corporal, and of such and such a sort. What is that, my well-beloved daughter? Ah! no, I desire that your cross and mine be entirely crosses from Jesus Christ.

—FRANCES DE SALES, *LETTERS TO PERSONS IN THE WORLD*

Mrs. Stalcup? This is Phylicia at Kaiser Permanente."

"No," I said in quiet desperation. "Please don't tell me it's positive again!"

"I'm afraid it is," she replied, sympathetically.

I dropped my head onto my desk. How long is this going to go on? I wondered. By now I could recognize the advice nurse's voice. She called every two weeks like clockwork to tell me that my nine-year-old son, Sammy, still had strep.

It had begun in early February. That first week, we were both sick. Sammy and I lay in my king-size bed in a fog of fever. On the second day, I dragged us both to the doctor. I had the flu and he had strep.

He took ten days of penicillin and bounced back quickly. I remained sick a week longer. But two weeks later Sammy was having odd symptoms. He had a rash on his legs and torso. Then a high fever. The next day, the joints in his legs turned bright red, as if they had gone to the beach without the rest of his body. Then his knees swelled to the size of cantaloupes.

His knees were so swollen they wouldn't bend, and he winced with each stiff-legged step. We took him back to the doctor several times before they discovered the problem. He had . . . strep. "How can that be?" I asked the doctor. "How can strep make his knees swell?"

"I'm afraid," she told us, "the strep has gone into his system."

We came home with a new prescription for penicillin. This time Sammy mended slowly. At the end of the ten-day prescription I took him in for another throat culture to confirm the strep was gone.

It wasn't.

The doctor prescribed a different antibiotic, but by now I was getting anxious. *Why wasn't God healing Sammy?* I had been involved in healing prayer for more than a decade, and had seen him heal many people, but my son wasn't getting any better. Our church was praying for Sammy, too.

One morning in prayer I heard God tell me, *Sammy will not die.*

Not die, I thought, alarmed. *What do you mean, not die? I didn't think he was going to die!*

But God didn't answer.

It made me wonder, *what lies ahead?* I was praying fervently and meticulously following the doctor's instruction, so when Sammy didn't get better I began to feel a simmering rage. *What did I have to do to get a healing?* Then my mind jumped to the thought that *I must be doing something wrong*—and like Job, I had lots of friends helping me feel that way. They would call with suggestions such as, "Why don't you put the dog on antibiotics? Why don't you submerge your bathroom—or, make that, your whole house in an immense vat of Lysol?"

Then there were the spiritual ones—"Betsy, have you searched your heart for any hidden sin?" Everyone assumed that I must be doing something wrong—*and I at some level thought they were probably right!* "Clean your house thoroughly," they said. "Have him suck on zinc lozenges. Have him gargle with saltwater." Their words hit me like stones raining down on my head.

I was trying to meet writing deadlines, tutor Sammy so he wouldn't fall behind in school, and take care of all the normal household chores. One night as I crawled into bed feeling as friable as a cornhusk doll, I complained to my husband, "Everyone keeps calling with advice as if it has become their job to fix us. I wish they would come clean my doorknobs, instead of telling me to clean them."

I was a rubber band stretched taut. Little cracks were forming along the edges. Any minute, I was going to snap, but I couldn't let up. What if one of their "suggestions" were the very thing that would, *violà,* make Sammy well? And I didn't do it because I got ticked and went to bed, when all that was needed was for me to spend ten minutes flossing the dog's teeth?

One morning in prayer God whispered to my heart, *You're not doing anything wrong.* This was good news—and bad. It was a tremendous relief to know that I wasn't doing anything wrong. On the other hand, it also meant that there was nothing I could do to fix it. No button I could push or doorknob I could swab to make Sammy well. I wanted control. But it eluded me.

If I am not doing something wrong, why isn't God healing my son? Deep down inside I was sure that God must be displeased with me. Years before my pastor had said, "Disappointment with God is his invitation to go deeper." So I went back on my knees and talked to God about it. What he said shocked me. He said, *Betsy, remember, I said 'no' to Jesus, too.*

In my mind I saw Jesus in the garden asking his father, let this cup pass. At that moment, I wasn't too sure about God loving me, but I was sure he loved Jesus, after all he was the good boy, the sinless son. Yet God said *no* to him, too. If that was true, then maybe, I wasn't doing anything wrong. Maybe God was simply saying no. Maybe he had reasons I couldn't understand.

I continued to monitor Sammy's health, his diet, and his rest. I continued to spoon in the medicine. I continued to take him in for a throat culture after each round of antibiotics. I couldn't tell if he was improving. He seemed tired all the time. Was it the strep or the antibiotics that were making him so listless?

Then a month later I heard God speak to me one more time. He said, *Not much longer.*

Oh really, I snapped. *What do you mean, not much longer? The Bible says that a thousand years is like a day to you! Long from whose perspective, mine or yours?*

Sammy had one more day of antibiotics. We waited 48 hours after the last dose and took him in for a post-therapy culture. Then we waited to hear from the advice nurse. I didn't have much hope that Sammy was well because he seemed so weak.

For three months, Phylicia, the advice nurse, had called us every other Tuesday morning. We had 10 days of antibiotics, two days of waiting, then a culture and 24 hours of waiting until results were available. I knew our HMO's policy: A call meant strep. No call meant no strep.

I was supposed to write on Tuesday morning while Sarah was in preschool, but I was so restless, it seemed as if my brain circuits were down. By eleven, Phylicia still hadn't called. *Could Sammy be well?*

My husband was calling me every ten minutes. Every time the phone rang, I jumped, thinking, *It's the advice nurse!*

“Honey, have you heard yet?” It was Sam. Again.

“Please stop calling me. I told you I would call as soon as I hear. Better yet, you call the nurse. I'm afraid to call, and you're driving me nuts!"

The phone rang ten minutes later. It was Sam. "He's well," he told me, his voice hoarse.

We cried together, holding our phones. At last, our son was well.

I learned so much through Sammy's illness. I remembered with shame the times that I had judged other people's pain. I was guilty, too; I had assumed that people in pain must have been doing something wrong. Now I knew that sometimes God calls us to suffer even though we have done nothing wrong. During my most desperate moments I would picture God's altar and cling to it. I held onto his altar when nothing else would help.

I thought back on my life. When I got pregnant out of wedlock, I suffered because of my sin. I expected my life as a single mom to be painful because I had to face the consequences of my sin.

When we moved across the country, I suffered because of my unbelief. If I had trusted God more, I would not have been in so much pain.

When I lost my job, I suffered because God took away something that I held dear and replaced it with something better.

During Sammy's bout with strep, I experienced the suffering of Jesus because I was criticized and rejected by those who loved me. In the book of Romans, Paul says that he wants to know the fellowship of Christ's suffering. Every time I read that passage my flesh cries out, *NO! I don't want to know your suffering.* Yet I am profoundly grateful for the sufferings of Christ because my wrestling with God brought me to a higher level of faith and freedom.

Although Sammy's strep disappeared that summer, by fall Sarah had three cases of strep, and was stricken three more times after Christmas. It was a rough year. Between the two children, we went through more than 17 rounds of treatment for strep in twelve months. But it was a rich year as God broke my heart, drawing near to him for comfort.

Pediatric oncologist Diane Komp, M.D., of Yale Medical School, says that the parents of young cancer victims often tell her that dealing with their child's cancer has changed their lives forever. They say, "Obviously, I didn't want my child to have cancer, but I wouldn't want to go back to being the person I was before this happened."

Those words express my heart. The fellowship of his suffering is rough, but honestly, I wouldn't want to go back to being the person I was before we went through all this. During that time, God birthed in me a new depth of compassion for those who suffer and a new understanding of his ways that has been so valuable that I can honestly say it was worth it all.

*****

Are you angry with God because your life is hard?

Dear Lord,

This is so hard! We keep getting hit by one thing after another. Financial setback, illness, and pain. Lord, have mercy on us! I know I shouldn't, but I get so angry. I thought you were supposed to be a loving God! You are the God of the universe, so surely you could change this if you wanted to. I know you must have a reason for this—help me to trust you. Give me a heart that is willing to share in the fellowship of your suffering because, right now, I don't want to have anything to do with your suffering. Change my heart! Break me, Lord, and make me willing to suffer for your sake.

In Jesus' name, Amen.

~ CHAPTER 3 ~

THE LIFE GOD HAS FOR ME

Every day we experience something of the death of Jesus, so that we may also know the power of the life of Jesus in these bodies of ours. Yes, we who are living are always being exposed to death for Jesus' sake, so that the life of Jesus may be plainly seen in our mortal lives. We are always facing death, but this means that you know more and more of life.

—II Corinthians 4:10-12 (Phillips)

Christ bids a man come and die, then he gives him the only life worth living.

—Dietrich Bonhoeffer

Is this the life God has for me?" I whined to my husband, Sam. I was weary and discouraged after Sammy's tonsillectomy. Sammy was in so much pain he couldn't sleep at night. He woke me up over and over again. After a few days I was so tired I had lost all perspective. Little did I know things were about to get worse.

"Sammy," I said gently as I put him to bed two days after his surgery. "I know your throat hurts, but tonight you have to sleep in your own bed. I am so tired."

"Sure, Mom," he said. "It doesn't hurt so much anymore. I won't wake you up. I promise."

I fell into bed that night and slept soundly until 4 a.m. I awoke. There was someone standing next to my bed. "I'm sorry, Mom," Sammy whispered, "but I have a bloody nose."

"A bloody nose?" I asked, reaching for the light. As I feared, the blood wasn't coming from his nose. There was blood on his mouth and along his jawline. "Sam," I woke my husband, "go get Sammy's pillow and see if there is any blood on it."

I dashed downstairs and snatched the post-operation instructions off the refrigerator. Yes, we were to call if there was any bright red blood.

A pool of bright red blood the size of a dinner plate had soaked through Sammy's pillow. I called the doctor.

By 5 a.m. we were on our way to the hospital. I sat in the back seat of the car holding Sammy's head in my lap, wiping away the blood with a bath towel as it trickled out of his mouth. The blood he had swallowed was making him nauseous, so I was trying to keep more from going down his throat.

We pulled up to the emergency room door. I hustled Sammy inside while Sam drove off to find a parking place. The doctor arrived at the hospital while the triage nurse was still taking Sammy's blood pressure.

"We need to take him back into surgery," he told us, grimly. Sammy turned to me, put his head on my chest and started to sob. I gulped down my tears and nodded. *Anything, I thought. Anything to stop the bleeding.*

A nurse started an IV line. Just before they wheeled Sammy into surgery, a phlebotomist came to take blood—or so I thought. Instead he used a small spring-loaded blade to stab Sammy's forearm, then he watched him bleed to see how long it would take him to stop bleeding. It seemed positively draconian.

Sammy bled for 15 long minutes.

"Less than seven minutes is normal," the doctor informed us. "This is way outside the range of normal." Then he continued, "We think Sammy may have von Willebrand's syndrome, a mild bleeding disorder that most people don't know they have until they hemorrhage after surgery. We'll have to keep him in the hospital."

I tried to be brave as I walked into the operating room with Sammy, wearing the bouffant cap, mask, and gown, but when the anesthesiologist clamped the mask down on Sammy's face I almost lost control. Though Sammy couldn't talk through the mask, his blue eyes seemed to plead, *Mom, make it all go away*. I felt helpless as I watched tears trickle down the sides of his face. Then the anesthesiologist injected a thick white serum into Sammy's IV line. In less than ten seconds, he was out.

I stumbled out of the operating room and leaned against the wall. In the distance, down the long corridor, I could see my husband waiting.

"Why," I cried, "Why has our life been so hard? Why is Sammy sick again? Why did he need a second surgery?" The first time, we had been prepared. Nothing had prepared us for this moment.

We huddled together in the quiet waiting room. The sun had come up. It was Saturday morning. People were trickling into the hospital. The sign on the espresso stand a few feet away said, "Hours nine to nine." I checked my watch. It was 8:00 a.m.

"Call someone," I wearily told my husband. "Ask someone to pray for us."

"Isn't it a little early?" my husband asked. Then he looked at my face, got up and walked to the phone.

By 8:30 a.m. the surgery was over. By 9 a.m. we were with Sammy in his hospital room. He looked pale and weak. He couldn't speak.

He motioned to me that he needed his inhaler. In the early morning rush to the hospital, I hadn't thought to bring it.

I went to look for the nurse. She listened to his lungs. He was wheezing. Now, on top of everything else, he was having trouble breathing.

My head began to pound. I curled up on the little bench seat in his hospital room, trying to stop the pounding, trying to gain control. I was getting sick to my stomach. My heart was sliding into a bottomless pit. *God,* I cried, *Help! I'm overwhelmed, I can't deal with this.*

My husband went in search of Motrin. One of the pediatric nurses brought me a handful of saltines. Another found a chair that unfolded into a narrow bed. She pulled it next to Sammy's bed. I crawled in and tried to block out the noise, the lights, my life.

An endless stream of people came into Sammy's room to draw blood, to give him breathing treatments, to check his IV. A pediatric hematologist came to talk to us about von Willebrand's. Had Sammy ever had bloody noses or bruised easily? The answer was yes.

They would treat him through his IV, then when we went home, we would have to give him 24 pills a day for the next 10 days—six at midnight, 6 a.m., noon, and 6 p.m. The pills couldn't wait, or he would hemorrhage again. We would have to wake him each night to give him his medication.

"Why don't you go home, take a shower, relax, then come back here to spend the night," Sam said. "I'll stay with Sammy until you get back."

As I drove home, I cried, "Why, God? Why?"

At home, I lay on the floor of my bedroom, exhausted, yet too tense to sleep. It was hard to think, to pray, to move. I lay there for several hours, partly awake, partly asleep, then I forced myself to get up, shower, and pack a small overnight bag for the hospital. Then I headed back.

Why? I asked God again.

Then he spoke. *There will be a great healing that comes from this.* I didn't want to hear this. I assumed that I would grow spiritually. I always did in painful situations, but at that moment I wanted it all to go away. I wanted it to stop now. I didn't want to grow. I didn't want to get another long drawn out healing.

I don't know what God meant by the words "a great healing," but part of me wanted to believe. Sammy endured six months of tests before the doctors knew what was wrong with him. By the end of July, we knew that he had von Willebrand's. We looked to God, trusting and believing, though we did not understand.

*****

Have you ever faced a terrifying loss that didn't make any sense?

Dear Lord,

Be near me. I am hurt and confused. I know you have all power. You could stop this in a moment if you wanted to. But for some reason, you are letting us go through it instead. I thank you for sparing my son's life. I thank you for good doctors and nurses. I thank you for healing medicine. Be near me. Calm my frantic heart. Give me your peace that passes all understanding.

In Jesus' name, Amen.

CHAPTER 4

HEARING THE VOICE OF GOD

Our problem is not that we doubt God's ability and desire to communicate, but we are all too easily stumped as to how to identify his voice.

—Charles Stanley, How to Listen to God

We should be profoundly grateful that Scripture is available to us as an objective foundation, especially in times of crisis when our own inner voice provides only a maze of contradictions that lead us into confusion and despair.

—Klaus Bockmuehl, Listening to the God Who Speaks

The Lord is a refuge for the oppressed, a stronghold in times of trouble. Those who know your name will trust in you, for you, Lord, have never forsaken those who seek you.

—Psalm 9:9-10 (NIV)

People often ask me; how do you hear God's voice so well? There is only one answer—lots of practice. In some ways, knowing God is like knowing anyone. As you listen, you learn to recognize their voice just like I recognize the voice of my husband on the telephone. I never mistake his voice.

I've spent a lot of time quieting and interacting with God. I almost always hear God's voice clearly now, but I can be wrong. When Sammy had his tonsils out, I heard a voice that I thought was God's, but wasn't. I was just leaving the operating room after they put Sammy under anesthesia, when the thought, *You're going to lose him,* popped into my head. I shuddered, then pushed the thought away as I stripped off my green surgery suit.

I never told anyone what I heard that day, but it planted a seed of doubt and fear in my heart. Three days after the surgery when Sammy started to hemorrhage, I thought of that voice. Had God been warning me?

Then the doctors told us they thought Sammy had von Willebrand's syndrome. During the painful days that followed, I thought more and more about that voice. Was it God?

I was afraid to tell my husband about what I had heard because I didn't want to scare him. One late night, in a vulnerable moment, I let it out. I was right, he was terrified.

It wasn't until weeks later that I realized for the first time that the voice wasn't God's. I was sharing what I had heard that day with the women in my Bible study group. "I'm still not sure if it was God's voice," I admitted.

"How did it make you feel?" my Lithuanian friend, Edita, asked.

"Terrified," I answered. Then, instantly, I knew. God doesn't terrorize his children. Even when his word is a hard one, we feel no terror when we hear his voice. It is gentle. Even if God had said, *Sammy is going to die soon,* there would have been peace and a sense that God was with me, a sense that I could trust God with my son's life.

That time, there was no peace, only a sick, cold dread. I had listened to the enemy of my soul and had lived in gut-wrenching turmoil because of it.

Thankfully, I had community that was able to help me see what was true and what wasn't. I had an ongoing relationship with God where I spent time in the Word and in his presence every single day. I often interacted with him and knew him, not just about him, *but him!*

I've experienced him quieting the voices in my head, the ones that say, *You're worthless. No one loves you and no one ever will. Your situation is hopeless.* I've seen him on the cross and I've heard him sing over me that I am his beloved. In my strong moments I know that I am precious to God and dearly loved.

I know because I know him through the Bible, through the church, and through experience. Over four decades I have grown more and more securely attached to him. We give our time gladly to that which we love. I read God's Word daily. I talk with him throughout the day. I have memorized Scripture so that it can pop into my mind when I need to recall its truths. I know God's character because we have an intimate relationship.

*****

Do you recognize God's voice when he speaks to you?

Dear Lord,

Draw me nearer to you. Help me to know your voice when you are speaking to me. Help me discern your voice from the other voices in my head. Take away my confusion, my fear, and my doubt. Help me to know you intimately so I can hear clearly and be quick to obey.

In Jesus' name, Amen.

CHAPTER 5

STEPS OF FAITH

Which of you, if his son asks for bread, will give him a stone? Or if he asks for a fish, will give him a snake? If you, then, though you are evil, know how to give good gifts to your children, how much more will your Father in heaven give good gifts to those who ask him?

—JESUS, MATTHEW 7:9-11 (NIV)

I do believe; help me overcome my unbelief!

—THE FATHER OF THE DEMON-POSSESSED BOY, MARK 9:24 (NIV)

Compared to our church in Fairfax, the church we were visiting was tiny. It held, perhaps, one hundred people, but they made up for their small size by their deep passion for God. Once a year we attended this church while we were away on our annual week at the beach. We enjoyed the lively worship and our kids liked the Sunday school.

That Sunday morning, at the end of the opening songs, the pastor turned to the congregation and asked, "Would anyone else like us to pray for them?" I glanced down at Sammy, who was standing at my side. "Do you want to go forward?" I whispered. He nodded his head, then started up the aisle with my husband, Sam. I lagged behind feeling a bit uncomfortable. By the time I got to the front, a small group had surrounded my son. Sam explained what was wrong with Sammy and the group began to pray.

I stood on the outskirts, squirming. I had asked God for strength, for mercy, and for an accurate diagnosis, but gradually I had stopped asking God to heal Sammy. The strep had gone away only to come back. The tonsillectomy that was supposed to solve

Sammy's health problems led to hemorrhaging, unmasking his bleeding disorder. I was afraid to ask; afraid of being disappointed again. I knew that Sammy desperately wanted to be healed so he could play football, basketball, and soccer but I was willing to live with the disease. At least life was stable. We had an accurate diagnosis and the doctor said, if we were careful, it wouldn't kill him. Deep down inside, I thought, *I can handle this.*

After they finished praying, Sam took Sammy off to Sunday School and I returned to my seat. As Sam was heading back into the sanctuary, someone in the back stopped him to say that there had been a prophesy earlier in the summer that there would be healings of cancers and blood disorders at that church in August.

It was August 2.

When Sam stepped into the pew and whispered this news to me, tingles ran up and down my spine. Could it be? Yet it was hard to believe after months of disappointed prayers that God would heal Sammy.

For several months I had sensed God whispering to my heart, *Why don't you ask me to heal him?* But I hesitated. *What if we asked and God said no?* A few times I had quietly prayed, *Lord, heal my son.* But I was afraid to earnestly intercede, I kept my thoughts frozen in my heart until one night, I shared them with my husband. To my surprise, he said he had been having the same thoughts. Gradually I began taking baby steps of faith and prayed, *Lord, heal my son.*

Was this the moment? I wasn't sure, but like Mary, I pondered these things in my heart.

Two weeks later, Sammy was scheduled for a treatment trial. The doctor was going to test various medications to see which one would stanch the bleeding quickest. Then Sammy was going to start carrying this medication with him 24/7—just in case he got in a car accident or accidentally cut his finger. The treatment trial would take most of the day. They started by testing his bleeding time. Then they would give him medication through an IV, followed by another bleeding time test. If the medication worked, his bleeding time would decrease markedly.

Dr. Horn snapped the spring-loaded blade on Sammy's arm, making the first cut, then watched the clock. One minute, two minutes, three, four, five, six, seven, eight. His bleeding stopped after only eight minutes.

The doctor was clearly dumbfounded. She looked from him to me, and back again.

A flame of faith began to flicker in my heart.

"What's going on?" she asked, looking from him to me and back again, eyebrows raised. I was speechless. Before, his bleeding time had always been much longer. "I don't know what do," she said, thinking out loud. "His bleeding time is almost normal."

"Mom, I keep thinking about those people who prayed for me in that church at the beach," Sammy said, as he sat up, too excited to remain prone. Sammy told Dr. Horn the story as I inwardly winced. I was afraid she would think we were religious fanatics, but she listened respectfully.

Dr. Horn decided to continue the treatment trial, but the results were inconclusive. After treatment, his bleeding time was six and a half minutes—within the range for normal, but not the dramatic decrease the doctor was expecting.

We left the doctor's office that day without a clear sense of what was going on. The doctor mentioned several options—including retesting him or going to a different lab to get tested—but the tests had been horrible. We didn't want to do that again. So we decided to wait a month and do another bleeding time test to see what would happen.

Meanwhile, my heart had come alive; my faith was igniting. *Lord, heal my son,* I cried. It didn't make sense. There were children with cancer who filled Dr. Horn's waiting room, but it looked like God might be healing our son.

When I got home, I called every prayer warrior I knew and asked them to pray. "I think God may be healing Sammy. Pray that he completes the healing."

*****

Are you willing to settle for second best? Is there a deep desire buried in your heart that you are afraid to take to God? Perhaps a marriage partner, a child, a healing?

Dear Lord,

Forgive my lack of faith. Strengthen my heart and give me the faith to share my deepest longings with you. I am so easily satisfied with second best, but you want the best for me. Take away my fear and help me to take hold of the good things you are doing in my life. Give me the faith to cry out to you. You have made me. You have placed these longings in my heart, and you want to fill them. Come Lord Jesus and fill my heart.

In Jesus' name, Amen.

~ CHAPTER 6 ~

HEALING ADVENTURE

December 1999

Lord Jesus Christ, Son of God, have mercy on me a sinner.

—THE JESUS PRAYER

If you make the Most High your dwelling—even the Lord, who is my refuge—then no harm will befall you, no disaster will come near your tent.

—PSALM 92:9-10 (NIV)

I was so restless, I couldn't sit still. In just a few hours, I was going to fetch Sammy from school and take him to see Dr. Horn for more testing. She had wanted to test him again in October, but I had put it off until soccer season was over. Since his bleeding time had been near normal in August, I had let him play. *What if his bleeding time is up again?* I wondered. *What if God wasn't healing him?* I knew it would break his heart to be pulled from the team in the middle of the season. So I buried my head in the sand and put the test off until the season was over. For months the cry of my heart had been, *Lord, heal my son.* In August, it looked as if God was healing Sammy. Today's appointment—a quick stab in the arm—would either confirm my hopes or send them spiraling down.

On top of the tension I felt over the upcoming test, I was having trouble with the referral. Though I had ordered it weeks before, it had fallen through the cracks, and now my pediatrician was out of town. All morning my pediatrician's nurse had tried to get the referral approved before my appointment, as required, but she wasn't making any headway against the HMO's bureaucracy. Now it looked like I would have to go to the hematologist without approval and hope that my health care provider would still cover the cost. This added to my turmoil.

I was jittery. *Should I cancel the appointment and reschedule? Was God trying to protect me from disappointment?* I prayed and prayed some more. *God, show me what to do. I am so scared. Give me courage. I know you don't owe me anything, but I want Sammy to be healed so much. Help me to accept your will.*

I decided to go. At least then we would know. *Lord, I prayed, show me mercy. Have them cover the cost.* I picked up Sammy and headed to the hematologist, 15 miles away. On the way, he had lots of questions: "If my bleeding time is normal will I be able to play football?"

"I don't know," I answered.

"What will we do if it is high?" he asked. "Will this be the last test?" Sammy wanted to nail down all the possibilities, but I didn't have any answers and his questions made my chest squeeze so tight it hurt. I wanted to listen and be a sympathetic mother, but what I really wanted was for him to stop asking questions. *Ahhh,* the dilemmas of motherhood—what makes you tense, makes your child tense so they come to you for reassurance—but you haven't any, which magnifies your tension—and their's. In the past I would have issued a withering blast, leaving my children too stunned to speak or even breath, but I had sworn that off for Lent, so I gripped the wheel and prayed for strength.

The wait in the doctor's reception room was always difficult. The doctors are oncologists as well as hematologists, which means they were cancer doctors as well as doctors who treat blood diseases. Many of the children in the waiting room were so thin and bald that their legs looked as if they had no flesh. I always feared

I would burst into tears if I looked at them too closely, so I tried to tune them out. Sometimes this was impossible as conversations between mothers and their children, so tender, so filled with poignant loss would break my concentration and burrow into my brain, breaking my heart as I sat buried in a book reading the same line over and over.

Why, I wondered, *would God heal my son when these children are so desperately ill?* Sammy didn't even feel sick. I looked around the room. To my left, a large boy—big enough to be a man, but still clearly young, sat next to his mother. His skin was completely white, a baseball cap covered his bald head.

None of the sick kids ever misbehaved. Their siblings could be so obnoxious that I wanted to scream at them, but the sick ones, and their parents seemed to dwell in a holy space where the parent-child bond was immutable, impenetrable, and saturated with love.

It seemed that every time we went there was an emergency—a kid who came in for treatment only to be taken directly to the hospital. I knew that our case was not desperate, so we waited.

The first time I took Sammy to see Dr. Horn, we had had a two o'clock appointment and still had not been seen by six. I had brought six-year-old Sarah with us, and by six o'clock all three of us were hungry and peevish. We hit McDonalds the minute we left the doctor's office, and even I, who abhor fast food, sank my teeth into a cheeseburger.

Now I knew better. When we went to the doctor, I brought good books and healthy snacks and left Sarah at home with Mina. Then we hunkered down to wait.

Today the wait seemed interminable.

Finally, the doctor called us. She prepared Sammy for the bleeding time test by having him lie down and asked me to read him a story to keep his mind off the test. I picked up Sammy's book, *Treasure Island* and started to read aloud. It seemed like the test was taking forever, but I forced myself to keep my eyes on the book and not on the clock because I knew that Sammy's eyes were locked onto my face and if I looked at the clock, he would too.

I was sure the test had gone well over twenty minutes, when Dr. Horn straightened her back and said, "Six minutes." I stared blankly at her. "Six minutes," she repeated, breaking into a wide grin. "His bleeding time is normal. It's gone. Whatever it is, is gone."

"Gone?" I asked in a daze. Even though I had longed to hear those words, it didn't seem real.

"Can I play football?" Sammy asked eagerly, swinging his legs over the side of the examination table and sitting up.

"Yes," she said. "All restrictions are lifted."

"When do we come back?" I asked.

"Never," she said. "You never have to see me again."

It was over. Sammy was well and we would not have to come back and endure that waiting room again.

As we were getting into the car, Sammy said, "Mom, this has been the worst year of my life, but I have grown so close to Jesus during this time. Now I hear his voice. He is so near to me now. I pray all the time."

Tears rolled down my cheeks. They were the words a mother longs to hear. Even without Sammy's physical healing, it had been "a great healing" for all of us. It had been worth the pain. Then to top it off, to make it even better, to put icing on the cake, God had healed Sammy physically, as well.

My heart will never cease to be grateful.

Author's Note: Six months later Sammy was back playing football. That season his team won the Fairfax County championship for their division. More icing on the cake!

*****

When a long trial is finally over the victory is so sweet. Can we thank him for it?

Dear Lord,

Lord, I don't know how to begin to thank you for bringing us through this trial. I can hardly believe it is over. You didn't have to heal my son, but you did. I want to thank you with all my heart for your mercy toward me and my family. Give us faithful and steadfast hearts that run after you all of our days.

In Jesus' name, Amen.

❧ CHAPTER 7 ❧

SAM'S TORN TENDON

I was desperate for you to help me in my struggles, and you did!

—Psalm 120:1 (TPT)

I am so very grateful that I serve a God who walks the difficult roads with us, whether we recognize him there or not. I am so very grateful for a God who has experienced betrayal, fear and death himself and overcomes them all.

—Joan Campbell, Encounters

In the middle of that dreadful season of sickness, when my two youngest children were nearly continuously sick, my husband Sam tore the tendon in his right middle finger. He had spilled a cup of coffee on the cream-colored carpet in our family room and was using a dish towel to try to soak it up. A dish towel is no match for a coffee stain, but he gave it all he had, rubbing so hard that his middle finger caught. He felt a sharp stab of pain and was astonished to see that he could not straighten the last joint of his middle finger. He could grab it with his other hand, push it back and pop it into place but as soon as he made a fist, it bent and would not straighten. That last digit remained curled. We went to the doctor and they diagnosed a torn tendon.

"These usually repair on their own if you keep it straight for six weeks or so," the doctor said. The nurse wrapped Sam's finger in a splint and sent him home with instructions to come back in six weeks. As I recall it was not a huge impediment. Sam no longer had to wash dishes, which made him *very* happy.

Six weeks later he went back to the doctor who took off the splint. He had him ball his fist and then open his hand and sadly the last joint of the injured finger remained bent. They put him in the splint for another 12 weeks or so, but the finger did not heal. On the third visit to the doctor, he said, "You're going to need surgery."

Sam has never been one to complain. But the night before his surgery I had a meltdown. I remember being in bed and telling God that I had had it! My husband, who falls asleep the moment his head hits the pillow, was snoring but I was not the least bit sleepy because I was so angry. *Wasn't it enough that my son and daughter could not seem to kick the strep?* After the surgery, Sam would be even less available to help around the house—or even pick up after himself. I sobbed as waves of hopeless despair assailed me. I did not have the capacity to take care of everyone, to help with homework, do the laundry, put meals on the table and work at the geological survey. I remember telling God, "I can't do this."

At the time I had no thought that my rants would change anything, I simply could not contain myself. Feelings were bubbling up and out. I was telling God, the only person who was willing to listen to me, that I simply could not face the future I saw before me. Years of childhood trauma had left me with intense unregulated emotions and at this point they were like a steam locomotive bearing down on my heart and mind. Sam continued to sleep—nothing wakes him unless I grab him and shake him. So, no one heard my cries but God.

I soon drifted off to sleep. There is nothing like crying hard to make you sleepy! The next morning the alarm blared about two hours earlier than usual because Sam needed to be at the surgery center by 7:30 a.m. As was his custom he sat up and swung his feet over the side of the bed trying to wake up.

I rolled over and closed my eyes, hoping to sleep a bit longer.

Then I heard him say loudly, "Look! Look!" I rolled back and opened one eye. He thrust his hand in front of my face. I struggled to focus. He made a fist and straightened it, then did it again and again. His finger was completely healed. My groggy brain could barely take it in. How could that have happened? Was he showing me the correct hand?

Then it hit us both: God. God had done this. I was overwhelmed with the awareness that God had done this for me. Yes, clearly also for Sam, but in that moment, it felt personal as gratitude for his love and care swept over me.

"What should I do?" Sam asked.

"I think you should go in. If you don't show up, they'll think you're a no-show and they might get stressed waiting for you since you're their first appointment of the day."

"You're right," Sam said, standing up. He pulled on the clothes he had laid out the night before. Soon I heard the car start in the driveway.

Within an hour he was back jubilant. "The doctor said it is completely healed."

That morning was more than 20 years ago, and he has never had a problem with that finger—no pain, no clicking or popping, no trouble opening or closing his finger. It works just like all the others.

We praised God for his faithfulness, his kindness, his goodness. He sees, he hears, he understands, and he is able to do something about all that weighs us down.

*****

Have you ever reached the end of yourself and cried out to God without much expectation that anything will change—and then it did?

Dear Lord,

Oh, ye of little faith. That would be me. I feel almost ashamed of last night's pity party. I sure got down to it, crying about it all and feeling overwhelmed. I am so grateful that I am your beloved and you are mine. You see my weaknesses with tenderness and compassion. I am grateful for your love and care. Help me to trust you more and more.

In Jesus' name, Amen.

CHAPTER 8

KEY IN THE SAND

August 1997

Every single moment you are thinking of me!
How precious and wonderful to consider
that you cherish me constantly in your every thought!
O God, your desires toward me are more
than the grains of sand on every shore!

—Psalm 139:17-18a (TPT)

I believe in Christianity as I believe that the sun has risen; not only because I see it, but because by it I see everything else.

—C.S. Lewis, quote on his memorial stone

"You what?" I asked, trying to keep the alarm out of my voice.

"I dropped the keys on the sand, back there," Sammy said, pointing up the beach.

"You what?" I asked again. My stomach knotted and my brain felt like cotton. But the answer was still the same.

"Where?" I asked

"Where we were standing before," my 10-year-old son replied. His wide blue eyes looked up at me, but I looked away, down the beach.

We were standing on Coquina Beach in North Carolina holding a wet, salty kite. We had been flying kites on the beach when one of the kites dove into the sea. It had been five hundred feet in the air when it plunged into the drink. For an hour, Sam, Sammy, Sarah and I had been slowly walking up the beach as I tugged gently on the kite string. As the sun sank in the western sky, we wound the taut string, tugging gently, slowly to keep it from breaking as the surf pulled it back and forth. At last we spotted the kite in the dark surf. Sammy waded into the water and grabbed it. We cheered. The main pole was broken, but the kite was saved.

Now it was dark. A full moon shone on the black water and gray-looking sand. At last, I thought, tired and hungry, we can go back to our beach cottage.

But where were the car keys? Sammy had had them last. He had used them to get the kite from our car. When I asked him for the keys, he told me he had dropped them in the sand back where we had been standing before we embarked on our kite-saving mission.

What could Sammy have been thinking? I asked myself. My husband and I looked at each other and shook our heads. By now the beach was deserted. Our car was the only one in the parking lot. The doors were locked. How would we get inside the car? How would we get back to the cottage, ten miles away? How would we get inside the cottage once we got there? Our days of renting beachfront cottages had disappeared along with my job as a scientist. The cottage we were staying in this year belonged to a friend who lived in Virginia, a five-hour drive away.

"Lord," I cried, "You've got to help us! We've got to find those keys!"

The four of us started walking back up the beach in silence. Sammy was sniffling.

We met fifteen-year old Mina who was sitting in a beach chair reading a novel in the fading light. "Mina," I asked, "do you have any idea where we were standing before the kite went down?"

'You've got to be kidding," she replied with a trace of sarcasm, as she tilted her head and arched her eyebrows.

When she heard our dilemma, her tone softened. "I don't know," she said looking around. "Maybe over there? I think my beach chair was here. Yes, here are the marks in the sand."

Meanwhile, we were praying out loud. Whining, really. We were whining to God.

"Wait," I told my husband, looking around. "I think I remember this sandcastle." There was a large lumpy sandcastle, broken by the waves, about ten feet further inland. By the shimmering light of the moon, I scanned the area. Then I spotted a solitary sandal lying on the sand. I remembered that sandal.

"I think we were standing in this area, between the castle and the sandal," I said. The ruined castle and lost sandal were about 30 feet apart.

By now, Sammy was sobbing. I did not know much about the importance of attunement back then and sometimes, I even thought people were supposed to suffer *to learn their lesson! Ouch!* "Sammy," I said, "please stop crying and help us look. Everybody come here and look." In the darkness, every shell and patch of seaweed on the surface of the sand looked like a set of keys. We walked slowly back and forth. Every few feet I bent over to pick up the keys, but it was always a shell, a bit of dried seaweed, a ghost crab shell, or a bit of trash. We searched for at least a half hour. Every few minutes I stopped and tried to comfort Sammy, who was sobbing. "It's okay, Sammy," I told him, "we all make mistakes," but inside I was thinking, *this takes the cake!*

I felt something crunch under my feet. It's just a shell, I told myself, like so many shells I have stepped on. But something made me think, *I'd better look. I want to be thorough.* I poked my finger in the sand. About half an inch under the surface I felt something hard. It was . . . THE KEYS. I could not believe it. I shook them in the darkness to be sure.

In the vast sea of sand, God had led me to step on my keys!

All I could think was, *How precious to me are your thoughts, Oh God, how vast is the sum of them.* God not only met our need; he showed Sammy that he could redeem our childish mistakes when we turn to him.

*****

Do you need a miracle? Can you cry out to God?

Dear Lord,

I am simply amazed. I know that you knew where those keys were the whole time—yet when you led me to step on them it boggled my mind. I wasn't expecting them to be covered by sand! I was looking on the surface. You are so wonderful. We are so thankful. Thank you especially for doing this for Sammy, to build his faith and show him that you can redeem our most ridiculous bloopers. I love you!

In Jesus' name, Amen.

❧ CHAPTER 9 ❧

SAM'S GOLD TOOTH

November 1999

The walk of faith is to live according to the revelation we have received, in the midst of the mysteries we can't explain."

—BILL JOHNSON, DREAMING WITH GOD

Then God added his witness to theirs. He validated their ministry with signs, astonishing wonders, all kinds of powerful miracles, and by the gifts of the Holy Spirit, which he distributed as he desired.

—HEBREWS 2:4 (TPT)

Charisma Magazine hired me to write a story about the gold manifestations that were happening all around the world in 1999. I was highly doubtful that they could be genuine, but I agreed since the location they wanted me to visit was a short drive from my home in Reston.

For six months, Charisma's offices had been flooded by fax and e-mail reports of gold dust falling on people during worship, as well as accounts of believers receiving supernatural dental healings. Silver amalgam fillings or crowns turned to gold or platinum, or even to white enamel. Others claimed they received new fillings or crowns that appeared in their mouths where they had had no previous dental work. And some said entire teeth had turned to gold.

When we pulled into the wooded parking lot next to Calvary Pentecostal Tabernacle in Ashland, Virginia, we could hear lively praise music coming from the meeting house—a wooden structure that seats more than 1,500 people. It was a sweltering summer night—with no air conditioning in the place. Even so people were singing, clapping their hands and dancing in the aisles. We grabbed our seats in the second row.

I had spoken by phone with Ruth Heflin, a 61-year-old Pentecostal minister whose family had preached at this camp meeting for 45 years, but this was my first time seeing her in person. I scrutinized her, searching for any trace of the supernatural gold dust. Despite the heat, Heflin was wearing a long-sleeved black dress. I watched her closely as she worshiped, and I saw no metallic gleam anywhere. But as the service progressed, tiny specks of gold began to appear, first on her face and then on her clothes. I remembered what she had said about the gold dust when we talked on the phone the day before: "It falls like rain, or it just suddenly appears."

I searched the air over Heflin's head. With its high ceiling and theater-style seats, the tabernacle was open on all sides to the surrounding woods. Occasionally I thought I saw something floating in the air, but each time it turned out to be a buzzing insect drawn to the bright lights. As I watched, more gold appeared on Heflin and on some of the women in the music team.

I was skeptical. After all, I had worked as a geologist for the federal government for 17 years. My scientific training told me this was impossible. *Lord,* I prayed silently, *If this is of you, I want to know.* A few minutes later I saw flecks of gold on the face of a teen-age girl a few seats away. Later, I spotted two tiny bits of gold on my wrist. Baffled, I held my wrist up to the light and twisted my hand back and forth so I could see the gold as it sparkled. Even though it was happening to me, it was hard to believe. Was God really manifesting the glory of his presence in this way?

The meeting went on for hours. I had brought my husband and three children with me, so when it got late, we made what we hoped was a discrete exit and drove to our motel room nearby.

In the morning my husband playfully teased, "Everyone check their teeth! Anyone have any gold teeth?" We all gave a laugh and opened our mouths. "Wait!" Sam said, shocked, "Is that tooth gold?"

I assumed he was joking and ignored him. But he insisted, "Betsy, look at my tooth!" He was pointing to a back molar. I could not see well, so I pulled him over to the bank of lights above the sink. I still was uncertain. "Come outside with me."

We were on the second floor of a motel just off route 95. Once we were in daylight I looked again. His tooth looked gold. As a geologist I knew what gold looked like, but I was not easily convinced. "Are you sure that tooth was not gold before?"

"Yes, I am sure."

Still I doubted. Sam was celebrating his miracle, but I needed more data to be convinced. When we got back to town we went to the dentist, who looked up his dental records. They showed that Sam had had a porcelain crown put on that tooth a few years previous. I still doubted. Is there any way you can get a bit of that gold off, without damaging the crown?

"Sure." Our dentist took a polishing tool in his hand and placed it by the tooth. For a brief instant the machine whirled, then he wiped the head on a piece of gauze and handed it to me. "Is that enough?" There were about 30 small flecks on the gauze.

"That works!" I said.

I called my friend Harvey at the Geological Survey. "I have two samples; can you tell me if they are real gold?"

An hour later I was at the Survey. Harvey loaded the samples one at a time in the scanning electron microscope. A sample a local pastor had given me was glitter. It sputtered and melted as soon as we dropped the electron beam. The sample of Sam's tooth was gold. Not just gold but *dental gold,* mixed with another element to make it harder, since pure gold is too soft to make good teeth.

I believed. I had taken my doubts to their limit and had to believe that God had turned my husband's tooth to gold. For years he delighted in showing people his gold tooth, which was not easy to see since it was so far back in his mouth.

Why did God turn his crown to gold? I have no idea! People I interviewed when I was writing the article named many possibilities. Some said it is was a sign that Jesus was coming soon or that revival was near or that God was simply displaying his extravagant love.

One South African man said, "I believe this is a sign to make people wonder. An outward and visible sign of an inward and spiritual grace." We need to "follow the sign to God and hear what he is saying."

For me, it built my faith when the unexplainable happened to us.

Sadly, for reasons that I do not understand, about a decade later Sam needed another root canal on that tooth and our dentist had to remove the crown. Knowing it was special to him, he gave it to him in a little bag. Sam still has the tooth.

*****

Is there something that you cannot bring yourself to believe?

Dear Lord,

You know my faith is small. I feel like the man who cried out, Lord, I believe, help my unbelief! Your ways are so beyond me. All I can do is worship you in your glory and transcendence. Teach me your ways! Open my eyes to know that you can do anything.

In Jesus' name, Amen.

CHAPTER 10

GOD HEALS BUSTER

2004

I sing because my soul is happy.
I sing because I'm free.
For His eye, it is on the little sparrow.
And I know He's watching over you and me.

—Mahalia Jackson

If it matters to you, it matters to him.

—Bill Johnson, Dreaming with God

It had happened once before, but this time surgery did not help. "Would you like us to put him to sleep?" the vet asked kindly.

I could not imagine letting go of my dog Buster, my first dog, a standard poodle that I had secretly purchased as a gift for my dog-loving family one Christmas. My husband wanted a dog and I was not open to the idea because my "to do" box was already stuffed tight. "No. No. and No." I said over and over again.

But I hate to say no to my husband. It gnawed at me. I went to the local library and check out a book entitled, *How to Choose a Dog for Your Family.* I hid it between the mattress and box springs knowing that if Sam knew I was weakening, he would bring home a dog. I decided on a poodle because three members of our family had asthma at the time and poodles were, according to the book, hypoallergenic—and smart. I found an ad for Standard Poodles in the Washington Post, and went by to see the puppies.

A few days later I asked my husband to take a ride in the car with me, before he left for work. I told him it was a surprise. When we were in the car, I confessed that I was willing to get a dog, but only this particular breed. When he heard the word "dog" he started to crow, but when he heard the word "poodle" he looked at me as if I was insane. "Poodle! You want me to get a poodle!"

"Yes," I answered trying to sound firm. "It's a big poodle. Well not now, but he will grow into a big dog and we don't have to give him a poodle haircut. He can look like a normal dog." By then we were turning into the breeder's driveway.

As soon as Sam saw the adult dogs, as large as labs, and the adorable puppies his heart melted. We paid for our puppy but arranged to leave him at the breeder's until Christmas Eve.

On Christmas Eve, on the way home from church, we told our children, "We have to go out again to pick up one more present."

My teenage daughter, the sole organized member of the family, gave me a scornful look as if to say, *You still have more shopping to do? Now?* But thankfully she did not say what her facial expressions so clearly expressed.

We rushed to the breeder's in the next town and came home bearing a white puppy. When we stepped inside the house our three children were playing a game on the floor.

They looked at me, holding the puppy in my arms. "Whose dog is that?" asked Mina.

"It is your dog!" I answered.

"Our dog?" they echoed in disbelief.

"Yes. Your dog!"

I put him down and the children ran to Buster and began laughing and petting their puppy.

As happens in so many families, I was the one who fed and walked the dog. I did not have a long commute and was working six hours a day, so was the one who was home more than any other member of the family, and in time although he was our family's dog, I was the one he followed.

Now, his gut was twisted, something that can happen to dogs with deep chests. "We've released the built-up gas in his stomach so he is not in distress right now, but it will build up again and he will be miserable. He cannot survive this," the vet explained.

I pondered my exceedingly narrow choices.

"Can I bring him home, just to say good-bye?" I asked.

The vet paused, then said, "Yes, we can let you have him overnight, but you have to promise to bring him back in the morning."

When I hung up the phone, loud, wrenching sobs came out of my body, noises I did not know I was capable of making. It was startling, even to me.

Why was I in so much pain? The answer came quickly, *my dog loved me unconditionally. No one else has loved me the way Buster did.*

Sam and I went to pick him up. He looked subdued though his tail wagged a little when he saw us.

Our three children gathered around him when we got him home. We were not allowed to feed him as the food would only come right back up again. Me being me, of course I prayed for him, but he would need a miracle to survive and though I longed for one, I did not expect one.

The next morning, he seemed energetic. Could he have recovered?

Then the vet called, "You promised to bring him in."

"Yes, I know but he is wagging his tail and seems so happy."

There was a long pause. "You need to bring him in. Don't wait until he is suffering."

I looked at my husband, lost. I shook my head. "I think he may be better," I said to the vet.

Her voice took on a tone that said that I was testing her patience. "Yes, temporarily but the gas and pressure will build back up."

"Okay, we will bring him back."

We said our tearful farewells. I opened the car door and Buster hopped in the backseat.

While Sam drove, I got an idea, I would ask for one more X-ray.

When we got there, I asked the vet, "Would you be willing to X-ray him one more time, just to be sure.

She looked doubtful.

"I will pay for it; I just want to be sure his gut is still twisted."

"Okay," she agreed. She led him back into the treatment area.

Sam and I waited and prayed. "Oh God, could you be healing our dog? Lord, come and heal our dog, help us to believe, help the vet to see what you are doing."

In what seemed like a very long time, she reappeared.

Somehow his intestines had untangled. "I don't know how that could have happened, but it has."

We cheered right in the waiting room and thanked God for his mercy on us. We took him home rejoicing in our miracle.

We had him for several more years, then he died of the same affliction. I did not cry the second time like I had the first. I had gone to God and received a deep healing for the pain that rose up when I thought we were going to lose Buster. I was slowly developing a secure attachment to God, an attachment that made it easier to trust him. I was experiencing God's unconditional love, in waves. The second time, it felt as if it was time, God's time, to let our dear dog go.

*****

Is there something in this life that you are so attached to that you can't imagine losing? Can you talk to God about how you feel?

Dear Lord,

I remember the day they told me our dog was going to die. Suddenly I was overcome by sob so loud that one of my family members came to the doorway and said, "What is wrong with you? It is just a dog."

With those words I sunk into shame. Then, my heart answered, *No, it is not just a dog, it is all the losses I have endured, all the people who misunderstood me or failed to accept me. My dog loves me just as I am.*

I thank you, Lord, for this unconditionally loving dog—one that I did not want yet won my heart by demonstrated your love for me in such a tangible way. Open my heart to be able to drink in your love for me. Help me to experience your unconditional love and to trust that you will always be here with me.

In Jesus' name, Amen.

❧ CHAPTER 11 ❧

FIRST CLASS

2005

Never doubt God's mighty power to work in you and accomplish all this. He will achieve infinitely more than your greatest request, your most unbelievable dream, and exceed your wildest imagination! He will outdo them all, for his miraculous power constantly energizes you.

—EPHESIANS 3:20 (TPT)

Waymaker, miracle worker, promise keeper, light in the darkness, my God, that is who you are!

—"WAYMAKER," LEELAND

We had had a wonderful vacation with my family in Sedona, Arizona and were now headed home. When we got to the airport in Phoenix, we were stunned to learn that our flight time had been moved up by several hours and had already departed. The airline had messaged me, but me being me, I did not check until after we received the bad news. Everyone was upset and fell to blaming, primarily me, and they had a point since I was the only one with a cell phone back then.

Then I had the thought, *Don't worry, good will come out of this. You are going to fly first class!* I was surprised and wondered, *Is this God? Or my own wishful thinking?* I was learning to distinguish my own thoughts from God's, and I suspected it was him.

Then I made a big mistake. I told my family what I was hearing and of course they mocked me. "Mom, really?" "There she goes again!"

When the airline booked us into economy seats, the family turned the whole thing into a joke. There are some spectacular mistakes I've made in my day and in moments like this the family loves to recount them. The time Mom killed the maple tree with her overzealous pruning. The time Mom poured salsa instead of spaghetti sauce on the spaghetti creating a completely inedible new dish. Then tried to serve it again when no one ate it the first time. Now they had a new family joke. "Yes, Mom thinks we are flying first class!"

Our new flight arrangements brought us to Las Vegas around 11 p.m. I remember opening my eyes long enough to see the neon lights, so blindingly bright in my sleepy state that they made my eyes sting.

We had to change planes. When we checked in for our next flight to Washington, D.C. they could not find seats for the five of us. I timidly asked, "What about first class?" Then the lady behind the counter paused, tapped a bit on her keyboard and said, "I am going to put you in first class." I smiled. *Had I heard right?*

Everyone looked at me speechless.

"How did you know?" they pestered me.

"I don't know! It must have been God." I suddenly had the energy to do a little happy dance.

We were going to travel in comfort on the longest leg of the flight, the red eye!

When we settled into our new seats close to midnight, we were tired, and the seats felt oh so comfy. As I closed my eyes and slept, I had the distinct impression that God was smiling at his little girl, *me!* And happy to have arranged all this simply to delight me and my dear ones.

*****

Have you ever thought God said something to you, but everyone around you made fun of you?

Dear Lord,

You are such a good father, so kind and loving. I can see you planning all kinds of special delights for us. Help us to notice and appreciate all the small "I love yous" in life such as first-class seats on a red-eye flight.

In Jesus' name, Amen.

~ CHAPTER 12 ~

STOPPING THE RAIN

September 2013

This father always relates to his children in perfect love. This father is never absent. He is never disinterested. He is never preoccupied. He is never unable to respond to a need.

—Henry T. Blackaby, Hearing God's Voice

Eye has not seen, nor the ear heard, nor have entered into the heart of man, the things which God has prepared for those who love him.

—I Corinthians 2:9 (NIV)

Rain! Was I imagining it? After all we were in Tucson, Arizona where it does not rain in September. Yet there is was, small but steady drops falling on all of us in our finery. We were seated at an elegant dinner, tables of eight, in the open central courtyard of a historic Pueblo. *Rain!* It was so absurd that people began to titter, then laugh. I looked over at the bride at the next table. A man in a tuxedo was holding an umbrella over her. But the rest of us were beginning to get wet. Some fished the decorative change plates under their real plates and held them over their heads.

Then the thought came to me, one of those thoughts that you know is not your own: *Command it to stop raining!*

Oh no, Lord, not now!

I was seated at the "Stanford" table with other graduates, between my husband and a man who was pioneering the use of satellite imagery to monitor the need for fertilizer for crops in China. He had been explaining his research to me, in fact, at that very moment he was still talking.

But there was the voice. I heard it again. *Command it to stop raining.*

I knew from past experiences that there was only one thing to do when God was telling me to do something I could not imagine doing—pray for strength and plunge ahead. I had disobeyed so many times and I knew that when I resisted or ignored his voice, I fell into confusion and doubt, uncertain if it was really him, upset with myself for failing to follow my master.

So I prayed, *Lord, help me!* Then I turned away from the man on my left, faced the middle of the table and said out loud, "In the name of Jesus, through the power of his cross and blood, I command it to stop raining!" I was firm. I was bold. Anyone at our table could have heard me, theoretically, but the only one who reacted was the man on my left. His head drew back sharply, his eyebrows shot up, and a look of incredulity crossed his face. Then surprisingly he turned to his plate and took another bite of food without saying a word to me. It was as if he had no place for such a message to land, so it just passed over him.

But there was one other reaction. It stopped raining.

Everyone cheered. The man holding the umbrella collapsed it. People resumed eating and drinking.

I was giddy with excitement. "Sam, Sam!" I tried to tug on my husband's sleeve, but he was engrossed in his conversation with the woman on his right and did not want to be interrupted. I persisted. "Sam! You've got to hear this!" He turned to me and I poured out my story. God had given me a part in stopping the rain! I felt like a hero! I was thrilled to have done my bit to save the dinner!

"That's wonderful," Sam said.

Later, out on the dance floor, I confessed to the mother of the bride, my dear friend from Stanford. She laughed when I told her what had happened just moments before. "Thank you," she said. "There was no plan 'B.' We had nowhere to go if it kept raining."

My heart was full of gratitude to God for his kindness.

* * * * *

Is there something that God is saying to your mind, something that you know is not your idea that you are resisting? Can you ask for help, then start moving forward?

Dear Lord,

Help me never forget the delight that floods my heart when you give me a role in what you are doing—and I do it. Forgive me when I resist. Please do not give up on me, keep talking to me until I obey so I don't miss out on those joy-filled moments!

In Jesus' name, Amen.

CHAPTER 13

IRANIAN NURSE

2010

You are the God who sees me," for she said, "I have now seen the One who sees me.

—Hagar to the Angel of the Lord, Genesis 16:13

Thou hast made us for thyself, O Lord, and our heart is restless until it finds its rest in thee.

—St. Augustine of Hippo, *Confessions*

The same year that my parents died, I was diagnosed with sleep apnea. Since I was not a typical candidate my doctor sent me for a CT scan, then to an ear, nose and throat specialist to see if sinus surgery could solve the problem.

When the nurse came to the door and called my name, something very odd happened. Something that has never happened to me before or since. As I walked towards the nurse, I saw the word "IRAN" in front of her. The letters were about the height of her shoulders. Each letter was about two inches high and looked like they had been squeezed out of a tube of smoke, a little wobbly but still clearly spelling out the word "IRAN" in white capital letters.

Without thinking I looked up into her eyes and asked, "Are you from Iran?"

She startled a bit then asked, "How did you know? Was it my accent? How did you know, do you have friends from Iran?"

I hesitated. She had only called my first and last name so I could hardly pretend that I had recognized her accent. I fell silent as we walked to the examination room.

As she wrapped my arm with a blood pressure cuff. I took a deep breath and told her the truth: "I think God told me. As soon as I looked at you, I saw the word, 'IRAN' written in the air in front of you."

She studied my face intently. Such dark intense eyes!

I asked, "Is there a reason God would be pointing you out to me? Are you in need? Do you need healing?"

"Yes." She said. "I am in need." Then she paused, and said, "I will be right back."

At this she bolted from the room. I heard loud heaving sobs coming from behind the door. *Oh no,* I thought. But as quickly as they began, the sobs ended and she appeared again, eyes red and swollen.

"I have been crying out to God," she said. "Just this morning I was in my car and I was crying out to God to help me, to give me strength. It is my daughter. She is my life. Right now, she is at Children's Hospital. She has to have surgery."

"God heard your cry," I said. "He sees you and he loves you." By now we both had tears in our eyes.

"Are you an angel?"

"Oh no, just an ordinary person! But can I pray for you and your family?"

"Yes, please do." I took her hand and asked her name. Parastu.[1] I prayed, "Dear God, you see Parastu and her family, you have heard her cry. Come and touch her. Let her know how much you love her and her family. Touch and heal her little girl, so that she does not need surgery. Draw near to her and give her your peace. In Jesus' name, Amen."

"I have to give you a kiss!" she said, bending forward to kiss my cheek.

"We have a healing service at my church this Friday," I shared. "I won't be there but if you go and take your daughter, they will pray for her." I fished out a card and wrote the time and day of the Father's Blessing, our church's healing service.

"I am not religious," Parastu continued. "I am Muslim, but not religious but I have been crying out to God. I have a good heart, I try, my husband and I try to do what is right. I am so blessed that God would have a message for me. My father died last year, and I asked him to stand between me and God." By now she was taking my blood pressure.

"We believe," I shared, "that Jesus stands between us and God, because of his sacrifice, his death."

She looked startled as if this thought had never occurred to her.

"Right now, my husband is with my daughter in Washington, D.C."

"At Children's Hospital?"

"Yes."

---

[1] Not her real name.

"Please let me know how it goes with her."

"I will. I am so grateful to meet you. I am so blessed."

It was many years before I found out what happened to Parastu's daughter. I had a dermatology appointment and as the nurse led me to the examination room, I realized that I was in the same suite of rooms where I had met Parastu.

"Is there a nurse, I asked, "named Parastu in this part of the building? She's from Iran."

The nurse paused and looked at me suspiciously as if she was trying to decide why I might be motivated to ask.

I hurried to fill in the blanks. "About five years ago her daughter was gravely ill and I prayed for her. But I never heard back."

"One moment," the nurse said as she stepped out of the room. Shortly she reappeared. "Yes, she is here and would like to see you. Don't leave until she is able to come."

At that point the doctor had not yet seen me, so I assured her that I would wait. The doctor came and went. A few minutes later Parastu stepped into the room and embraced me. "Yes, yes! My daughter is well! Thank you for praying for us." She then proceeded to list a number of other things she would like me to pray for as if I were a magician. I told her I would pray, silently praying that she would come to know Jesus relationally, as he is not a genie that grants our wishes.

Still. Still. It was a first step not too different from my own first step where I thought that if I pleased God he would grant me my heart's desires. I still pray for Parastu as she comes to mind. I trust this was one step in her journey towards the God who made her and is always drawing us to himself.

* * * * *

Have you ever had something strangely supernatural happen in your life, something that rattled you a bit, yet brought you joy?

Dear Lord,

Forgive me for being so timid. This was something that only you could do! And you let me play a part which brought me such joy and delight. Help me to trust that it is your heart's desire to reveal your true self to the whole world and to draw each person to you. Help me to do my little part well and trust you for the outcome.

In Jesus' name, Amen.

❧ CHAPTER 14 ❧

THE WATERFALL

Spring 2018

I am my beloved's and my beloved is mine!

—SONG OF SOLOMON 6:3 (NIV)

No one loves me like you. No one loves me the way you do.

—"NO ONE LOVES ME LIKE YOU," JARS OF CLAY

The Lord is my best friend and my shepherd.
I always have more than enough.
He offers a resting place for me in his luxurious love.
His tracks take me to an oasis of peace, the quiet brook of bliss.
That's where he restores and revives my life.

—PSALM 23: 1-3A (TPT)

I was lying in bed unable to sleep, a little frustrated with myself for being sleepless when I needed to rest. "What am I supposed to do?" I asked God.

Why don't you go back to the waterfall where you first started spending time with me?

In my mind I returned to the waterfall. I pictured floating on my back in the pool at the base of the falls. Jesus was in the water with me smiling and guarding me, so my head did not strike a rock as I floated. I had spent many hours here over the years, floating in the pool. It was here in this healing place that I began to recover from my fear of water and trust Jesus to watch over me. Then, as had happened many times before, we got out of the pool and climbed up the vertical cliff on the left side of the falls. We were both dressed like park rangers in shorts, shirts and sturdy shoes. He climbed behind me protectively with his arms almost around me to shelter me lest I fall.

I enjoyed the feeling of using my muscles. I have always loved to climb.

At the top of the falls we stood on a rock shelf, falls at our back and looked at over a vast plain. We had stood at this spot before.

My mind went back to the first time. We had stood watching tens of thousands of people march towards us, in step, resolute. The first time they had locked gazes with me, and I had become completely unnerved. I remembered asking Jesus, "Why are they looking at me?" His mouth curved into a calm smile. "They can't see me yet."

They clearly could see me.

As they approached, the front of the great throng vanished from sight. I anxiously looked at Jesus, what was I supposed to do? He looked down at me reassuringly but did not say a word. Then the first one was over the top, a ragged looking man, desperation lined his face. He headed straight towards me! I looked up at Jesus, who calmly handed me the most beautiful loaf of bread. The bread was golden brown, warm and smelled like rosemary. It was rectangular and large about twelve inches by eight inches by six inches. I thrust it into the hands of the man who was now just an arm's length away. His eyebrows shot up in astonishment, he gave a startle, took a little hop, pivoted and left. Then the next man was upon me. Again Jesus handed me a loaf and the whole scene repeated. About ten people, all men, came to me and Jesus had a warm loaf for each one. Then they stopped. We quietly walked over to the end of the cliff and looked out. The crowd had settled into groups of 50 or 60 and were all eating the bread.

To me the message was clear, feed the leaders. Feed the leaders. If you feed the leaders, they will meet the needs of their people and all will be satisfied.

Now we were back in that same spot. Again a sea of humanity was marching towards us. But now there were ten times more! My heart began to race. Jesus began to remind me how he had supplied loaves of bread and I had handed them off—one at a time—to the first ten people to reach us. He was saying, *Don't be afraid, I can do it again.*

Then he turned towards me, pulled me towards him, holding me with his hands around the back of my waist, and looked into my eyes. Then he began to sing to me:

I am yours and you are mine, We belong together!

I sang back, "I am yours and you are mine."

Then in a beautiful duet, our voices rising, *For we love each other*

"You are my God and King," I sang to him.

You are my sweet Betsy! He replied.

"Your love makes my heart sing," I sang back.

Nothing can harm you. He replied.

The song went on and on. So many verses, each one exactly what I needed to hear. I was filled with an inexpressible longing, a longing that was being completely satisfied for the first time.

I began to shake, laughing and crying in waves. Until that moment I had not realized how deeply I had felt rejected. In an instant, I saw how deeply I had been rejected as well as how deeply I was loved, *by him!* There was a place where I belonged, and it was with Jesus. All of me. The fear that I might overwhelm those I loved was gone. I could not overwhelm him. He was "all in." The thought, *I have been longing for this my whole life,* flooded me over and over again as I cried and laughed at the same time.

Then he said, *You can give me all your pain.* I saw a fountain of water shooting out of my torso and into him, rushing water cleansing me, as my pain flowed into him.

I was shaking so violently that I was vibrating our king-sized bed. Sam awoke, "Are you okay?"

I was unable to respond. I could hear the question, but I was in another realm.

Then the intensity of the vision faded enough for me to speak. I tried to find words to describe what I had just experienced. "I am having an encounter with the Lord. He is singing to me!" Then I sang the song to my husband. "That is the most beautiful song I've ever heard," he told me.

Jesus was still interacting with me, telling me that he was pleased that I care so deeply for people, that I loved like him but that *love does not need to be mixed with fear.*

This was profound. I love, but I worry. I began calling out names, surrendering people to him, starting with my children and extending out to almost everyone I know. Sam joined in and for more than an hour we were calling out names, out loud, to Jesus asking him to bless, to touch, to deliver, to heal. It was so sweet because we sensed that in that moment, we had a powerful anointing to call down blessings, healing and deliverance on people.

From the place in my vision, I could see the floor of heaven come low over the entire region. I could see through the translucent floor into heaven and those in heaven could see what was happening on earth.

I was afraid to go to sleep; afraid I would forget the song. I grabbed my phone and recorded what I could remember. Later the next day I got in touch with a musical friend and asked her to help me transcribe it. She came over a few weeks later and we worked on it but it was not until several years later that I actually got the score for the music and amazingly enough she had another musician friend compose accompaniment. Once again, the song brought a sense of profound belonging.

I belonged to God. I was his. It was as if he was my one true love and I was his.

There had been times in ministry sessions where I had seen others encounter God in this way. In the moment it feels as if we are his one and only, his bride, his beloved.

The astonishing thing about God is that each one of us is truly his favorite. Unlike human relationships, God has the capacity to be fully present and completely attentive to each one of us—at the same time. The attention and love he gives me does not in any way detract from the attention and love he is able to pour out on you. We tend to think of God's love the way we think of human love, but humans are so limited, and God's love has no limits.

*****

Even now, God is asking, may I sing over you?

Dear Lord,

Let me find your love irresistible. Open wide my heart and let me receive all the love you have for me, so I can trust you fully and feel your delight over me. I invite you to touch my deepest longings.

In Jesus' name, Amen.

Thank you for reading this slice of life from Elizabeth Stalcup, Executive Director and founder of Healing Center International, where we share the joys and sorrows of life with joyful leaders who know they are loved by God.

You can find out more at www.GodHealsToday.org.

Other books by Elizabeth Moll Stalcup

Whispers in the Storm

When storms gather in one man's body and he goes from being healthy and strong to close to death, chaos and destruction can quickly ensue. Not so with the Stalcup family, friends, and the medical community as they marshal their efforts to fight for Sam's healing and restoration. At the center of it all is God, who consistently reveals that he is there with them in every moment. He proves to be their faithful provider—pouring out grace, comfort, and much-needed healing for many at every turn. God's power and perfect timing are evident as the Stalcups go from the brink of despair to the heights of joy and hope. Your faith will be enriched as you walk through their experience in the pages of this book.

Crossroads Before Me

Alone. Frightened. And forced to choose—God's way or my own? Join Elizabeth's journey in her new inspirational memoir Crossroads Before Me. With openness and transparency, she chronicles her early years, writing for all who have felt the anguish of a broken heart and all those searching for the path to healing and transformation.

Made in the USA
Middletown, DE
03 July 2020

10935570R00050